INDIGENOUS BIOGRAPHIES

Billy Frank Jr.

Treaty Rights Activist

FOCUS READERS
BEACON

by Katrina M. Phillips

www.focusreaders.com

Focus Readers is distributed by North Star Editions:
sales@northstareditions.com | 888-417-0195

Produced for Focus Readers by Red Line Editorial.

Photographs ©: Ted S. Warren/AP Images, cover, 1, 13, 22; Shutterstock Images, 4, 8; Northwest Indian Fisheries Commission/AP Images, 7; MOHAI, Anders Beer Wilse Photographs, 1988.33.215, 10; US Fish and Wildlife Service, 15; Corbis Historical/Getty Images, 16; MOHAI, Seattle Post-Intelligencer Collection, 1986.5.56319.1, 19; MOHAI, Seattle Post-Intelligencer Collection, 2000.107.096.09.01, photo by Howard Staples, 20; National Archives, 25, 29; Alex Wong/Getty Images News/Getty Images, 27

Library of Congress Cataloging-in-Publication Data
Names: Phillips, Katrina M. author
Title: Billy Frank Jr: treaty rights activist / by Katrina M. Phillips.
Description: Mendota Heights, MN: Focus Readers Beacon, [2026] | Series: Indigenous biographies | Includes bibliographical references and index. | Audience: Grades 2-3
Identifiers: LCCN 2025012055 (print) | LCCN 2025012056 (ebook) | ISBN 9798889984993 hardcover | ISBN 9798889986539 paperback | ISBN 9798889985624 pdf | ISBN 9798889985310 ebook
Subjects: LCSH: Frank, Billy, Jr., 1931-2014--Juvenile literature | Nisqually Indians--Biography--Juvenile literature | Indian activists--Biography--Juvenile literature | Indians of North America--Legal status, laws, etc.--Washington (State)--Juvenile literature | LCGFT: Biographies | Literature.
Classification: LCC E99.N74 P45 2026 (print) | LCC E99.N74 (ebook) | DDC 973.04/97940092 $a B--dc23/eng/20250416
LC record available at https://lccn.loc.gov/2025012055
LC ebook record available at https://lccn.loc.gov/2025012056

Printed in the United States of America
Mankato, MN
012026

About the Author

Dr. Katrina M. Phillips (Red Cliff Ojibwe) is a writer, researcher, and history professor. She's written several children's books about Native histories and cultures, including *Indigenous Peoples' Day* and *I Am on Indigenous Land*. She and her husband live in Minnesota with their two sons and their goofy dog.

Table of Contents

CHAPTER 1

The Right to Fish

In 1945, Billy Frank Jr. was fishing for salmon on the Nisqually River. He was 14 years old. Billy was a **citizen** of the Nisqually Indian Tribe. He knew he had the right to fish in the river.

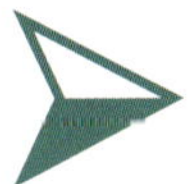

The Nisqually River is home to five types of salmon.

Billy caught a few salmon that day. He was happy. He knew the salmon would help feed his family.

But two **game wardens** were nearby. They said Billy was fishing illegally. The wardens tried to arrest him. Billy resisted. The wardens pushed him down in the mud. Then

Did You Know?

Billy Frank Jr. was arrested more than 50 times during his life.

Billy Frank Jr. (left) fishes in the Nisqually River under risk of arrest during the 1960s.

they arrested him. It would not be the last time Billy was arrested for exercising his **treaty** rights.

CHAPTER 2

Growing Up Nisqually

Billy Frank Jr. was born on March 9, 1931. He grew up on the Nisqually **Reservation** in Washington State. He lived on his family's land. It was a place called Frank's Landing.

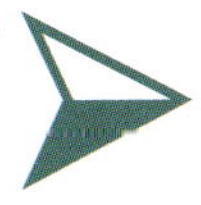

The Nisqually River flows 78 miles (126 km) from Mount Rainier into Puget Sound, which connects to the Pacific Ocean.

By 1900, Seattle, Washington, was a major center of the salmon fishing business.

Billy often fished with his family. Fishing was important for the Nisqually. They had fished in the area for thousands of years. But non-Native **commercial** fishers came in the 1800s. They often took more fish than they needed.

As a result, there were fewer and fewer salmon.

State officials responded. They targeted Native fishers. Officials claimed that Native people were fishing out of season. They claimed that Native people were fishing without licenses.

Did You Know?

The Nisqually Reservation was created in 1854 through the Medicine Creek Treaty.

The Franks knew their right to fish. But state officials disagreed. Billy's father, Willie, was arrested when Billy was young. Officials claimed he was fishing illegally.

Willie refused to give up. In 1937, he won a legal order against the state. This meant Nisqually people could fish without getting arrested. But the order lasted for only seven years.

The Franks continued to fish. Billy attended school through ninth

Billy Frank visits the Nisqually River at Frank's Landing in 2005.

grade. Then he started working during the day. He fished at night. Frank joined the US military in 1952. He served in the Korean War (1950–1953). He came home after the war ended.

TOPIC SPOTLIGHT

Treaties and Treaty Rights

The Pacific Northwest is home to many Native nations. Many signed treaties with the US government in the 1850s. The government often pressured Native nations to give up their lands. Native people were forced onto much smaller reservations. But these treaties protected Native rights to fish on these lands.

The Nisqually people were among those who signed treaties. One of these treaties was the Medicine Creek Treaty of 1854. Three more treaties were signed in 1855. They are the Treaty of Point No Point, the Treaty of Point Elliott, and Treaty of Neah Bay.

In 2016, Native nations met where the Medicine Creek Treaty was signed in 1854.

CHAPTER 3

The Fish Wars

Through the 1900s, Washington State passed more laws to stop Native people from fishing. Law enforcement arrested Native people for fishing. They even destroyed people's fishing nets.

Many Native nations in Washington State traditionally depended on fishing.

Native nations fished to provide for their communities. If they couldn't fish, they wouldn't survive.

By the 1960s, Native people had had enough. They started holding events called fish-ins. They were based on **sit-ins**. These protests were part of the **civil rights movement**.

The first fish-in happened in the early 1960s. It took place at Frank's Landing. Native people gathered to fish. They knew they might

Indigenous protesters held fish-ins along the Columbia River and along rivers that flowed into Puget Sound.

be arrested. But they knew they had to protect their treaty rights. Native people also held protests at the state capitol. The fish-ins and protests became known as the Fish Wars.

Young people from the National Indian Youth Council made up an important part of the Fish Wars.

Billy Frank Jr. helped lead the fish-ins. But he was not alone. Women such as Janet McCloud helped organize them. Sometimes the fish-ins turned violent. In 1965, game wardens rammed their boat into a fisher's canoe.

The Fish Wars brought attention to Native issues. In 1970, the US government sued the state of Washington. Four years later, Judge George Boldt made his decision. He ruled that the treaties protected the rights of Native nations. He ruled that they had the right to fish.

Did You Know?

Frank's sister, Maiselle, was also a leader in the Fish Wars. Her daughters participated, too.

CHAPTER 4

A Lasting Legacy

The Boldt Decision changed the lives of Native people. The ruling also led to a new group. It was called the Northwest Indian Fisheries Commission (NWIFC).

Billy Frank Jr. looks at photos of the Fish Wars in January 2014.

In this group, Native nations work with Washington State. Together, they protect natural resources. The NWIFC supports Native nations' treaty rights in Washington. Billy Frank Jr. was its first leader. He served in this role for more than 30 years.

Frank spent the rest of his life fighting for treaty rights. He also looked out for the salmon. He knew that **climate change** could harm the fish. He knew pollution could, too.

Chairman Billy Frank Jr. speaks at a Northwest Indian Fisheries Commission event in 2006.

Frank worked to protect the salmon and their homes.

Billy Frank Jr. died in 2014. He was 83 years old. He had received many awards during his life. And he continues to be honored today.

Native nations in Washington celebrate his birthday. The day is called Billy Frank Jr. Day.

The fight for treaty rights is not over. Native people still work to protect these rights. They call on the government to keep its promises. Like Billy Frank Jr., they remember the treaties.

Did You Know?

In 2021, Washington State decided to put a statue of Frank in the US Capitol.

After his death, Frank was awarded the Presidential Medal of Freedom. His daughter-in-law accepted the honor from President Barack Obama.

Focus Questions

Write your answers on a separate piece of paper.

1. Write a letter to a friend explaining what you learned about treaty rights.
2. Would you have taken part in the fish-ins? Why or why not?
3. How old was Billy Frank Jr. when he was arrested for the first time?
    - **A.** 14 years old
    - **B.** 50 years old
    - **C.** 83 years old
4. Why did Frank keep fishing if he knew he might be arrested?
    - **A.** He knew he had a treaty right to fish.
    - **B.** The number of salmon was increasing.
    - **C.** State officials wanted to let him fish.

5. What does **organize** mean in this book?

*Billy Frank Jr. helped lead the fish-ins. But he was not alone. Women such as Janet McCloud helped **organize** them.*

A. to buy food
B. to follow the law
C. to lead events or groups

6. What does **celebrate** mean in this book?

*Native nations in Washington **celebrate** his birthday. The day is called Billy Frank Jr. Day.*

A. to get older
B. to honor
C. to ignore

Answer key on page 32.

Glossary

citizen
A person who is a legal member of a certain nation.

civil rights movement
A mass struggle against racial discrimination in the United States in the 1950s and 1960s.

climate change
A human-caused global crisis involving long-term changes in Earth's temperature and weather patterns.

commercial
Done for the purpose of selling or doing business.

game wardens
People who make sure fishing and hunting laws are followed.

reservation
Land set aside by the US government for a Native nation.

sit-ins
Protests in which people refuse to leave places until specific changes happen.

treaty
An official agreement between two or more nations.

To Learn More

BOOKS

Lindstrom, Carole. *We Are Water Protectors.* Roaring Brook Press, 2020.

Phillips, Katrina M. *Native Hunting and Fishing: Practicing Traditions and Defending Treaty Rights.* Lerner Publications, 2025.

Sorell, Traci. *We Are Still Here! Native American Truths Everyone Should Know.* Charlesbridge Publishing, 2021.

NOTE TO EDUCATORS

Visit **www.focusreaders.com** to find links and resources related to this title.

Index